What people say

"Working with Dave and utilizing his particular knowledge of the rental market ensured we were successful from Day 1."
— *Paul, Room to Breathe*

"Dave's experience and knowledge of the property market helped my company source our first holiday let property and take it through the planning stage quickly and efficiently."
— *AH, Clear Property Group*

Praise for *Painless Property Investing*

"Once we had read Painless Property Investing, the fear of buying the wrong house in the wrong area vanished and, after further support from Dave, we bought our first investment property with plans for more to come."
— *Brian & Miriam, Bedfordshire*

"I suffered from fear of committing, but once I had read the book and understood the process, I was more certain and was able to begin building my own income producing portfolio."
— *NW, St Albans*

Painless Property Investing

A simple 4-step process to grow your own portfolio.

Dave Thomas

First Printing: 2023

Copyright © 2023 by Dave Thomas

All rights reserved.

Version 0.3

Cover design by Ken Leeder

This book or any of its parts may not be reproduced or used in any manner whatsoever without the express written permission of the author and publisher. However, brief quotations in a book review or scholarly journal are permitted.

Authors and their publications mentioned in this work and bibliography have their copyright protection. All brand and product names used in this book are trademarks, registered trademarks, or trade names and belong to the respective owners.

The author is unassociated with any product or vendor in this book.

Contents

Introduction	23
Purchase	31
Refurbishment	53
Rent	69
Refinance	83
Rinse & Repeat	95
Final Thoughts	99
Appendices	103
Appendix 1 – Six Sources of Seed Capital	*103*
Appendix 2 – The Four Profit Levers In Property Investment	*106*
Appendix 3 – PRRR and Flipping	*109*
Appendix 4 – Full Worked Example of One of the Author's PRRR Purchases.	*120*
Appendix 5 – Alternative Forced Appreciation Method: Title Split	*123*
References	125
One Last Thing…	127
Index	128

Disclaimer

The information provided in this book is intended for general informational purposes only and should not be considered as professional financial or investment advice, The author is not a licensed financial advisor and the content presented herein does not constitute a client-advisor relationship.

Property investment involves inherent risks, and the outcomes of investment decisions may vary based on individual circumstances, market fluctuations, economic conditions and other factors beyond the author's control. Readers are strongly advised to consult with qualified financial professionals, including, but not limited to financial advisors, tax experts and legal counsel before making any investment decisions.

The author disclaims any responsibility or liability for any actions taken by readers based on the information provided in this book. Readers are solely responsible for conducting their own research, due diligence, and risk assessment before making any financial or investment choices. Any reliance on the content of this book is at the reader's own risk.

Property and financial markets are subject to change and past performance is not indicative of future results. The author does not guarantee the accuracy, completeness, or timeliness of the information presented, and no warranties of any kind are implied.

By reading this book, readers acknowledge and agree to the terms of this disclaimer. It is recommended that readers seek professional advice tailored to their specific financial and investment situations before making and decisions based on the content of this book.

Free Gift!

As a "thank-you" for buying this book, I'd like to give you a free report that will reinforce much of what is included in the book.

10 Common Mistakes People Make When Investing In The UK Property Market.

Go to davethomasproperty.co.uk/Free_Report then add your details and this will be sent out to!

Enjoy!

Acknowledgements

Firstly, let me thank my wife, Janice, for her patience with me as I've been penning this "masterpiece". Watching me as I scribble down my thoughts on property investing, mainly on the beach at St Jean de Monts on the Vendee where my pen was fueled by the gorgeous lunchtime Rose wine, then, as my steady but slow one finger typing dropped these words into the current format and finally giving me a big smile as I held the first copies in my hand.

My heartfelt thanks must go out to Chris Payne, my mentor, for his help, patience, training and cajoling in helping me get this book completed and published. Since I first spoke to him about my book ideas over 3 years ago, he has always been there with constructive and, of course, correct comment on my ramblings.

He really made me believe writing a book was possible with his wonderful short book programme and, after I wrote and self-published my very first offering of "That Moura Moment", I was totally and utterly hooked and wanted to not only be a published, but best-selling author. Here's hoping!

I bet my good friend and neighbour, Bryan Hawley, regrets the day he told me he had been a proofreader in a previous life before retirement. Thank you for your talent and making this book as good as I hoped it would be.

I appreciate greatly the help of my close friend and business partner, Paul Jones, in offering to read through what I initially told him was a 25-page short book about property. He spent many hours, more than I think he anticipated, on his daily commute in the train from his home to his place of work in Stevenage, red pen in hand, marking up my technical errors and suggesting subtle changes for better effect in the content. I thank you!

Special thanks must go to Ken Leeder for his wonderful work on the designs for the book front and back covers, much appreciated, and to my illustrator, Gian Caneba, for the various drawings and cartoons dotted throughout the book. Without you two guys, the content would not have been so visually interesting.

I would also like to thank all the people who are too numerous to list that I've met on my long property journey; some good people and some not-so-good (you know who you were and probably still are!), over the past 17 years. I think I am getting better in my choices with people though as there does not seem to be many, if any, of the latter types in my circle of acquaintances anymore!

Finally, to all my readers (and I hope there are readers?), thank you for buying my book and I really hope it will encourage you to take the first tentative steps into property investing. If you enjoy it only half as much as I have over the years, then you will have a great time.

About the Author

Dave Thomas is an experienced UK property investor and has over 17 years and numerous properties under his belt. He is currently investing in the North of England.

He is very open to helping others on their journey and is happy to assist newbie investors where he can!

He is always looking to work with joint venture partners on opportunities on various Buy To Let and Holiday Let properties he uncovers so, if that is of interest to you, please drop an email, to dave@davethomasproperty.co.uk and explore the options.

To all struggling or aspiring property investors out there – this book is for you.

Introduction

Chapter 1

Introduction

> *"Everyone wants a piece of land. It's the only sure investment. It can never depreciate like a car or a washing machine. Land will double its value in ten years. In less than that. Land is going up every day."* – Sam Shepard

When you see all these property mentors and gurus talking about their 100+ residential Buy To Let (B2L) portfolios all at the regulation 75% Loan To Value (LTV), do you ever wonder where they found the minimum 25% to buy each of them in such quantity?

And how can you ever match this level of investment?

Well, worry not, as they have all, without exception, utilised this tremendous method of Purchase, Refurbish, Rent, Refinance (PRRR) investment to build their portfolios!

PRRR is a relatively low-risk strategy which has been proven, over time, to work and be highly successful. The basic premise is that the value of the property is increased by carrying out refurbishment, a process known as forced appreciation, enabling you, on refinance, to withdraw all, or the majority of, your money out of the deal.

This money is then utilised to secure the next deal, being used for the deposit and refurbishment costs through to a refinance allowing you to move on and buy further properties without the need for any further significant amount of money.

The holy grail of PRRR investment is to have a No Money Left In (NMLI) situation so that all of your investment money is reclaimed for reuse. In reality, at the time of writing, most deals are being done with some money having to be left in them.

The absolute nirvana for property investing is not only to get all your money out, but to also get out an additional tax-free surplus on your remortgage deal.

But don't worry, this money can still be recovered further along your property investment journey via subsequent refinancing cycles. More about that later!

The success of this strategy is illustrated by the fact that all the professional and sophisticated property investors have utilised these principles for many years enabling them to build their multi-million-pound portfolios from, possibly, one initial single deposit pot.

Then, as they have developed and grown their portfolios over the years, they have developed, in effect, after many refinancing cycles, a No Money Down (NMD) high cash-flowing portfolio where they have withdrawn any cash available as equity in the respective properties which has been used for growing the portfolio or as "fun money" in some cases.

So now, by following the steps and tips in the relative chapters that follow, you too will be able to copy and succeed with their methods.

In each chapter, the basic principles are outlined and some pitfalls to be avoided are also laid out. There are also several top tips included throughout to help you make the best-informed decisions when buying your own residential investment property.

The Author's Story

When the author started his property investing journey many years ago, this process did not have a specific name or title, as now, but was viewed as good, common-sense property investment strategy. Over the years the market leaders and the gurus have managed to develop some degree of mystique about the whole process and have created the acronym PRR to give it a scientific basis.

> To the author, it still makes sense, no matter what market you are in, to buy for the correct price, repackage and thus create a higher-value product!
>
> At the start, when building his portfolio and using the principles expounded in the following chapters, he tended to look for the cheapest option without, in many cases, considering the long-term implications of each purchase. This did lead to some costly rationalisation of the portfolio over the years to create the more robust and income producing one that he now owns.
>
> Now he tends to focus his property searches to family let properties that meet several important criteria in towns where rental demand is high and property prices are conducive to long-term growth. There is more detail about this buying criterion in Chapter 2, Purchase.

There does seem to be a current sweet spot for properties in this specific area, where the rental returns and the Return on Capital Invested (ROCI) are at a maximum, of between £70-£150k per property. This is, of course, after your PRRR upgrade had been completed.

But, in the right situation, you should be looking to buy properties in suitable areas that meet the criteria outlined in Chapter 2, Purchase, even if there is no room for forced appreciation of the property as it will still be a good purchase for your portfolio, but maybe not a great one.

Purchase

Chapter 2

Purchase

"Price is what you pay, value is what you get." – Warren Buffett

What Is My Strategy?

It is all very well deciding to become a property investor, but the type of property to purchase is not the first thing to consider. You must first decide what **TYPE** of property investor you want to be.

There are only five options available to you as anything else is a subset of one of the following and these are:

1. Buy to Let or Family Let (or B2L)
2. House of Multiple Occupation (or HMO)
3. Holiday Let (or HL)
4. Serviced Accommodation (or SA)
5. Rent to Rent (or R2R)

Of these, the first three are those which primarily lend themselves best to the PRRR process. Option 5 is not a purchase opportunity, but a property management option with cash flow but no capital growth element.

In practice most new investors always start with the Buy to Let strategy as it is the easiest to learn and operate and usually requires the least start-up or seed money to enable you to begin investing.

Buy To Let Investing

Under the whole gamut of Buy to Let there are further numerous subsets which need to be considered including:

- Two-up, two-down terraced houses which used to be referred to as "grunts" as being the basic building block of many portfolios
- Flats, both purpose-built or converted houses, usually with a lease and associated Ground Rent and Service Charge obligations which can eat into your profits
- Family lets which are usually considered to be three or four bedroom houses.

With the first two of these, the number of bedrooms, usually a maximum of 2, limits the size of the family that can live there and therefore, as the family grows, their housing needs change and they look to move on.

To avoid the transient nature of these properties, buying the larger-style family homes allows families to grow in your property and they begin to see it as their home and, in the main, take responsibility for it and will stay as your tenant for many years.

Note that each time you have a tenant change, there will be a void period where no rent is received and, no matter how nice the tenant has been, there will be deep cleaning and decoration touch up to do during the changeover which costs you money and time. Therefore, the longer a tenant stays in your property, the better it is for you financially.

> **Top Tip**
> **Don't buy because it is easy, buy because it works!**

Find A Motivated Seller

When looking for a property suitable for the PRRR strategy, finding a motivated seller can speed up the whole process in 2 ways:

1. More willing to allow negotiation to achieve a lower purchase price which will give you more headroom when you come to the Refinance stage.

2. Unlikely to be any chain involved so a simple process.

There are a number of different types of motivated sellers. These include:

- Distressed Seller
- Distressed Property
- Management Issues
- Investor Exit
- Lack of Owner Interest

Distressed Seller

Again, there are many different types of distressed sellers, each with their own set of issues, and they are usually under tremendous pressure to sell and to sell fast. They may already have tried the companies who guarantee to buy your house but have realized the huge drop in price that is being offered does not help them in their particular situation.

As long as you are not greedy, you can help them and be their saviour. Remember, you are a solution person, how can you solve their problems in a fair and ethical way?

The reasons why people are under this pressure to sell can include:

Repossession & Debt; they may be days away from repossession of the property and are looking for a solution that will both stop the process and allow them to walk away with a relatively clean credit record.

Divorce; when this happens and both parties, especially if children are involved, need to buy new homes, there are opportunities here to achieve a discount and get a quick sale as you are able to turn the deal around quickly and help both parties move on.

Probate; when an older family member dies, the property monies, when sold, will be shared between the heirs, all of whom probably have their own homes and would not be interested in moving into this house. Here, being in a position to move fast can give you a great advantage and enable you to generate a good discount on the sale.

> **Top Tip**
> Remember, you are a solutions person. How can you help solve their problems?

Relocation; people securing a new job, having to move away from the area and looking to buy near their new location are usually happy to accept a discounted price to speed up the sale.

Health Related; families moving a parent into a care home or a hospice, and requiring the money for the care almost immediately, are another area to explore and they will accept a discounted price for a speedy conclusion.

Retirement; much like relocation, a couple moving away for retirement are more likely to accept a discount to achieve the sale, enabling them to move sooner.

Finding out if a seller does come under any of these categories can be found by questioning the estate agent directly or asking the seller some pertinent questions when viewing the property.

Distressed Property

Here, when we are talking about a distressed property for a first-time investor, we are not talking about no windows, no roofs, no floors, in fact no house apart from four walls, we are talking about the internal features and decoration.

Most distressed properties have seen no updating or modernization for many years and some crucial indicators are some, or all, of the following:

- Swirly, multi-coloured patterned wallpaper throughout the house

Purchase

- Heavily patterned and dark-coloured carpets and thin, cheap linoleum in wet areas
- Polyurethane ceiling tiles
- Avocado bathroom suites or similar
- Dark-coloured paint on wooden surfaces
- Overgrown front and rear garden areas

If you view a property like this, control yourself as you have found the ideal PRRR property. But you need to assess the cost of refurbishment and make your offer only after consideration.

Ideally what you are trying to buy each time is the worst house in the best street as this will give you the greatest headroom when it comes to refinance and improve your chances or getting all of your money, and maybe a bit more, out of the deal.

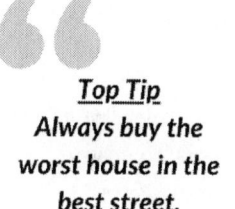

> **Top Tip**
> *Always buy the worst house in the best street.*

Your offer will only be "Subject to Survey" and you need to get your builder into the property and get his feedback in case there may be something crucial that you missed; or you can pay for a Homebuyers Survey (usually £250-400) where they will visit the property and give you a good, all-round report of the condition usually including their own valuation and estimates for the various items needing work.

Never rely on the survey for the mortgage company, for which you are required to pay, as that is for the lender's protection not yours and they will not necessarily point out anything wrong, just assess that the value is sufficient to cover the mortgage loan should you have to sell or default for whatever reason.

Management Issues

Here, armed with your extensive knowledge of your particular area, you can very quickly identify any properties where there seems to be an error with the pricing.

This is usually due to the seller engaging an agent from outside the general area, either physical or web based, with no specific knowledge of property prices who has set the price too low.

Getting in quick on a deal like this can be very advantageous to the investor.

Investor Exit

As with all occupations, some people get to an age when they decide to retire as a property investor. Although they probably know all the tricks of the trade, they may still be willing to negotiate a discount when they have made up their mind to go.

In fact, if they have more than one property, they may be looking to sell them all and this would give you a chance to buy a ready-made small portfolio to add to yours. This type of sale saves you a lot of time and effort as well as being very rewarding.

Other reasons for investor exit could be:

- Looking to change their strategy and move into other property types so need to sell to buy more.
- They may have had a larger tax bill than expected so need to get some quick cash in to pay that down.

Lack of Owner Interest

Some people, on inheriting a property from their parents, might have decided to give renting a try, but have then found that it is not as easy as it might have seemed at first glance.

These people are known in the trade as Accidental Landlords.

So, after their first bad tenant or their first big repair bill, they decide that it is not for them so a sensible offer to a landlord in this situation can bring the property under your control.

> **My First Property**
>
> When doing my initial research in my chosen Gold Mine area in the North-East, I found a 3-bed property for sale at £26k and thought to myself, what could possibly go wrong!
>
> I used the whole gambit of tools available to a PRRR practitioner during my research and this property came up trumps on many of them. Motivated seller (probate sale), distressed property (lots of old and outdated features) and an area where massive growth was planned (Council Redevelopment Zone). And of course, the top tip of "worst house in the best street", both of which were true at the time of purchase.
>
> The property was in an area of this North-East town where major redevelopments were being planned in both housing and infrastructure and the road on which the house was located, was designated in the plans as a major factor for access to the redeveloped area. They had even built a state-of-the-art police station at the end of the road with CCTV towers covering the immediate locality (shame they never

had enough staff to keep it open or man the monitors!)

My first visit was an eye opener as the previous owner, now deceased, had covered over the small open yard at the rear with acrylic roof sheeting and converted the area to be his kitchen. It was raining when I viewed the property and rainwater was dripping onto the electric hob below, not a great situation and would definitely need major modifications in order to pass any regulations!

There was an overpowering smell of damp in the property and there had been numerous attempts to cover it up but no investment to cure it.

Other similar houses in the street had been sold for around £42k and there were others on the market then at around the same price.

I still made a cheeky offer of £23k to gauge the interest of the family to sell, but it was made subject to survey.

Within 20 minutes, my offer was accepted and I engaged a local specialist to carry out a full damp and rot survey to find out the cost of the works needed.

From the results of this, I reduced my offer to £21k and it took a little longer, 40 minutes, for the revised offer to be accepted.

I found a recommended local builder and we agreed a price of £18k for all the work including a new roof.

Ten weeks later, the property was finished with a new damp course, new roof and tastefully decorated throughout in neutral colours with white gloss woodwork and doors.

The most expensive property in the street had been sold for £46k, but my valuer determined that, due to the high quality of the refurbishment, he would value the property at £54k.

With a 75% LTV mortgage, they advanced me £40.5k so, after covering all my costs and expenses and paying off the original mortgage, I was left with a small tax-free cash surplus of around £1000.

Cha-ching!

Now for the rental situation!

The highest rent seen in the street had been £405 pcm, but I put my property on for £465 pcm. I had many interested viewings by potential tenants and was able to rent it for the full asking amount one day after all the works had been completed.

With the mortgage being £185 pcm and other expenses of £80 pcm, my gross profit was £200 pcm!

Another Cha-Ching!

And, of course, by now I had my second and third PRRR developments under way!

Purchase Power Team

In this phase of the PRRR process, you will need a team of competent people around you and to assist you to make it all happen quickly and easily. This will consist of:

- Solicitor
- Surveyor
- Builder
- Mortgage Broker

Solicitor

Don't just phone up the first one you find on the web and engage them, you need to interview a number and find one that you (a) feel comfortable with; and (b) fully understands your plans as they will, ideally, also be a property investor.

They and their conveyancing team are critical in your moving with speed on the purchase and giving the vendor confidence on your ability to buy the property to meet their timescales.

Surveyor

If you are new to property, viewing properties with an eye for the cost of refurbishment then you need to either have a professional surveyor carry out what is known as a Homebuyer's Survey which will give you a detailed breakdown of the condition of the property with, in many cases, the likely cost for putting these right and also a valuation of the property.

Builder

If you have already identified a builder to carry out your upcoming refurbishment, then, rather than using a surveyor, you could visit the property alongside the builder and develop a list of works from that.

Mortgage Broker

A good, specialist mortgage broker is necessary for your success and when looking for one always ensure that they, and the company for which they work, has access to the whole market.

Many brokers are tied in to one or just a few mortgage companies so they will only be able to offer you deals available from these companies, thereby restricting the deals that you can access.

> *"Buying real estate is not only the best way, the quickest way, the safest way, but the only way to become wealthy."*
> *– Marshall Fields.*

Where Do I Purchase?
Where Is My Gold Mine Area?

Over the years, this has been a thorny question as some people like to buy a property close to their own home as this allows them to self-manage the property and keep an eye on both their investments and their tenant.

But this restricts you in your growth and could also restrict your income going forward by investing in what you think is the right area for you but not the right area for maximum profits.

You need to look further afield and if the best properties for return on your investment are 100 miles away for example, you need to do your research and buy there.

To find the ideal town, or towns, where you should begin to build you investment portfolio, there is a simple set of steps, or processes, to follow to identify not only the town, but the streets within that town where you should be investing.

As stated previously, your ideal town(s) are called your **Gold Mine Area** as by searching and digging, you will turn up some real nuggets.

You are looking for a town or large suburb with a population in excess of 80,000 as this ensures that there will be a relatively high number of families preferring to rent rather than, or be able to afford, to buy. These people will become your target market.

The current sweet spot for values in these areas is between £70-150,000 so looking more at the bottom end will highlight the PRRR type of properties and indicate the range to which the price can be lifted once your work has been done.

Then you need to narrow down where in your ideal town, your ideal residential properties will be located. As has already been pointed out, your target market is families so they will probably have a set of criteria of their own which will be their deciding factor so you need to determine what these are and find properties in areas that match them.

The work has been done on that front for you and these include:

- 3- or 4-bedroom houses with a garden
- Within 5 miles of the town or city centre

- Within 2 miles of infant, junior and secondary schools with a good or excellent Ofsted rating
- Close to public transport (bus and/or train) with direct access to the town or city centre
- Close to, but not on top of, a good local and national road network
- Walking distance to local shops

You will probably find two or three local postcodes that satisfy this list of criteria and then you can actually find the perfect streets on which to concentrate your property search.

> **Outsourcing Database Research**
>
> When I am looking to move into what I believe is a potential new area, I utilise the services of a VA (Virtual Assistant) usually based in the Philippines to do the initial database search on Rightmove.com for me.
>
> I developed a process document that lists all of the steps outlined above, with copies of relevant screen shots, that they are expected to carry out and then they supply me with a list of all suitable properties in my chosen area that meet these requirements.

> I now use virtual assistants I find on Upwork.com and they return a detailed spreadsheet to me in no more than two days.
>
> My next step is to extend the scope of this document to include the price analysis steps and rental incomes to reduce my potential opportunities to a more manageable number, all of which meet my criteria.
>
> This allows me to spend more time on IGTs (Income Generating Tasks) rather than basic database searches.

How Do I Buy?

As with any normal residential house purchase, there is a requirement for a deposit and then a balance payment - usually a mortgage - and for buying investment properties, the model is the same.

For your first portfolio property, as we are talking around the £100k mark including refurbishment, you will be looking for, say, £25k for deposit with £2k to cover fees with the refurbishment costs on top.

This money, or seed capital, will have to come from your savings or other means as will the refurbishment money. For an initial investment like this you are probably looking to have to hand around £37k which is a decent amount of cash to find.

If you are concerned how to fund your first deals, see Appendix One – Sources of Seed Capital, where a number of alternative approaches are offered.

Now, with the mortgage, you will be looking for one that has no ERCs (Early Repayment Charge) as these are levied by the mortgage lender and can be quite harsh, destroying any "profit" you may have made with your refurbishment project. They do this to keep the payee tied into their product for longer periods and not switching out to a cheaper loan every time a new one comes to the market.

But the very essence of what we are trying to do is to move on to a new lender at the earliest possible opportunity once we can get the house refurbished and revalued at a much higher figure. It is therefore imperative that your broker is fully aware of your plans and will find the best deal for you that has no ERCs. You may pay a higher rate of interest each month for this type of deal, but it will still be less than the costs of breaking the deal down the line.

Refurbishment

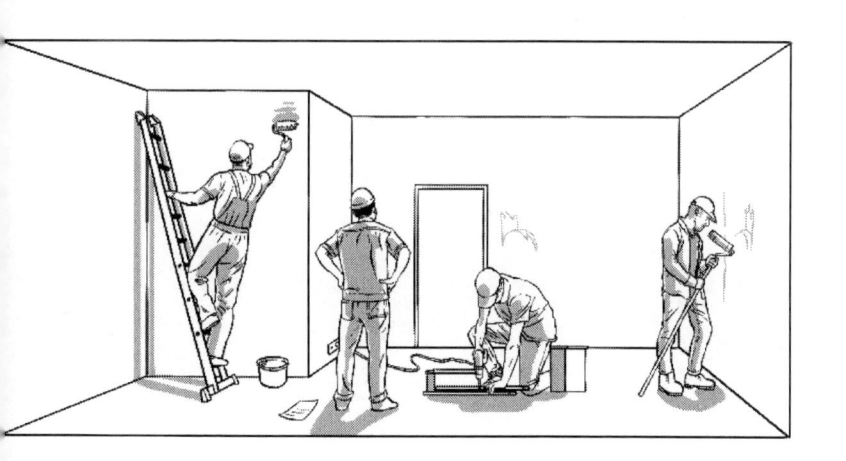

Chapter 3

Refurbishment

"Renovating not only restores the house but restores the story of the home and neighbourhood."- Anon

Refurbishment is an area where many investors, especially first-time investors, tend to spend too much and do more than is necessary for the property in question!

The first thing to remember when doing any refurbishment is that this is a rental property and not your own home. Too many people spend money on things for which they will never get the necessary return on items they have, or would like to have, in their own homes. They look to spend excessive amounts of money on things that the renters do not expect, including:

> **Top Tip**
> *Refurbish to the right standard for the tenant. Not the standard for you to live there!*

- Large flat-screen TVs in many rooms
- Fitted white goods in the kitchen
- Hive utility controllers
- Etc.

All of these can be part of the renters' own additions to the property, should they so desire!

Types of PRRR projects

In the author's opinion, there are fundamentally two different types of PRRR projects requiring different sets of skills and expertise. These are:

- **Cosmetic PRRR**
- **Structural PRRR**

These are explained below in more detail for what constitutes each type, but, unless you are already in the building trade or have a lot of experience in your own home of extensions, etc. The new property investor looking to use this PRRR principle to quickly build their own portfolio should cut their teeth on two or three cosmetic-style projects before branching into the more intense structural types.

Refurbishment

Cosmetic PRRR

My definition of a cosmetic PRRR is one where the investor/developer can go into the property and, in three months or less, make significant visual changes to increase the value substantially.

Here, when we are viewing properties with a mind to carry out this type of PRRR activity, we should be looking out and finding some, and hopefully all, of the following features:

- Swirly, multi-coloured patterned wallpaper throughout the house
- Heavily patterned and dark-coloured carpets and thin, cheap linoleum in wet areas
- Polyurethane ceiling tiles
- Avocado bathroom suites or similar
- Dark-coloured paint on wooden surfaces
- Overgrown front and rear garden areas

Finding properties with some or most of these old-fashioned features, will lead to a whole upgrade without the need for any major building works.

The work needed will include the following:

- Decoration throughout in bright and neutral colours
- Flooring replacement and upgrade
- Refurbishment or replacement of kitchen

- Upgrading of bathroom suite
- Tidy up of outside areas, front and back

Structural PRRR

This definition relies on major building works to gain a major uplift in value. This can range from a new roof, double glazing throughout, splitting one large room into two, extensions and even loft rooms.

With work like this, there may also be a need to apply for planning permission and/or building regs before the work starts and only your experience will tell you, when viewing, what is needed and then how long that might take to be given.

Unless you are starting out from a background in the building trades or have done this work in your own home, these types of projects are best left until you have gained more experience of the building trades and project management.

These are all large jobs, probably not suited to the novice property investor as delays at any stage of this work can seriously impact your cash flow and your end profits.

When looking at properties, you should try and see this type of added potential in any viewing. For example, many older 2-bed properties in the North of England had 1 large bedroom at the front and one at the rear with a bathroom downstairs. These large rooms usually have 2 windows, and these lend themselves to splitting to create a three-bed property with the bathroom moved upstairs as most people now prefer that type of layout. The extra space downstairs can become a utility room and still incorporate a downstairs WC, another bonus for a family let.

Refurbishment Power Team

In this phase of the process, the power team required is quite small, namely just the following:

Project Manager

If you are not able to keep a regular oversight on the refurbishment work, you may wish to employ a project manager to carry out weekly checks on progress and report back to you.

The company who did not get the work is someone you can ask to do this for a set fee each week and it means that you are on top of the work without the need to travel to site every time you want to gauge progress.

General Builder

Unless you want to manage a number of different trades and co-ordinate their efforts, the use of a general builder to do the whole job is probably the best option.

The company might not have all trades working directly for them but will have access to and can co-ordinate the work of the various tradesmen to ensure a speedy and efficient refurbishment.

What Are The Main Areas For Refurbishment?

The 4 major areas in which your refurbishment money should be invested are:

1. Decoration
2. Flooring
3. Bathroom and toilets
4. Kitchen

Each of these areas should have enough of the "WOW" factor for your potential renters that they are only too willing to pay the top price rent that you will be asking for the property.

When you are proficient at this refurbishment process, carrying out the necessary works at a suitable level on a standard size three-bedroom house should be able to be done for around £8,000.

By working closely with you chosen builder, shopping for the best deals and negotiating well, this should be easily achievable.

Refurbishment

Your first property might cost you more than this however as you learn your craft and gain experience, it will prepare you better for your subsequent properties.

Decoration

The major consideration here is to decorate the property in one neutral colour throughout to allow the renter to make their own subtle changes to turn the property from a rented house to their "home".

This is achieved by painting all the walls, after any building works have been completed, with a plain colour throughout. The favourite colour used to be magnolia as it was a bland colour and easily repainted, but there is so much variety in paint colours these days that any plain, neutral colour will suffice.

> **Top Tip**
> *Every £1 you spend on refurb must add £3-5 to the overall value*

All doors and other wooden items should be painted in a gloss brilliant white, as this gives a clean and refreshing look to all wooden surfaces. Using gloss on wooden surfaces also enables easy cleaning.

By leaving the house in a neutral state for your tenant, they can then repaint where desired, add feature walls using paint or wallpaper to create a property style that suits them and their lifestyle. They should discuss with your letting agent their choices before starting to ensure that there will be no issues later should they move out.

It is advisable that they are discouraged from painting the property in any dark or strong colours such as blacks and purples as these can be extremely difficult to cover between tenancies. They may say that they will return the property to the original state should they move out, but in most cases this is rarely done!

Flooring

If you have managed to find your potential property with swirly carpets throughout, now is your chance to replace then with a product, or products, to satisfy the rental market.

Let's first look upstairs where the bedrooms and the main family bathroom will be located.

When you get out of bed on a cold winter's morning, how nice is it to feel the warmth and comfort of a carpeted floor under your bare feet?

Although there is not a great amount of footfall in the bedrooms and the upstairs areas, it is advisable to go for a good quality carpet complete with an underlay. Many merchants usually include the underlay and the gripper bars with the price of the carpets especially if you are fitting out a whole new house. This double layering has two great advantages:

- To give a good "feel" as you walk on a carpeted floor.
- Reduce noise transmission through the ceilings to the rooms below.

The carpet chosen still needs to be hard-wearing and a neutral colour to match the wall colouring and with a fleck throughout to minimise any marks or dirt in use.

For the bathroom area, a good quality, hard-wearing patterned cushioned vinyl is recommended. Here some colour can be introduced as, in the next section, an all-white bathroom suite is recommended so this colour splash will break up the white tiles and bathroom items.

Another inexpensive way to bring some different colours into a bathroom is to add a vertical line of contrast tiles behind the taps and shower unit.

Some people recommend wood flooring in bathrooms, but unless you go to the top of the range options, there is always the risk of water damage causing lift and splitting of tiles. Vinyl is a cheaper option should you need to replace any damage.

Bathroom and Toilets

Hopefully, in your property search, you have uncovered an old avocado or brown bathroom suite that had done the previous owners proud for 20+ years, but now needs to be brought up to date for the modern, discernible renter.

The current best option is an all-white suite with white tiling and the rest of the walls painted in waterproof paint, probably in a brilliant white. This allows you to make quick and easy repairs and replacement of broken items as white is a universal colour when it comes to bathroom suites.

3-Bedroom Property

The ideal scenario here would be a separate WC with a wash basin with a second room having a bath, a wash basin and a walk-in shower unit as many families now prefer showers to baths.

But most properties come with a single, family bathroom consisting of a WC, bath and wash basin.

When you are changing the suite as part of your refurbishment, you should also incorporate a wall-mounted shower unit either off the bath taps or as a separate electric unit and provide a screen door in the shower area to minimise spray onto the floor or, at the very least, provide a rail from which a shower curtain can be hung.

4-bedroom property

Ideally there should be a downstairs wc with a fully fitted family bathroom upstairs as outlined above. Again, if there is space, an en-suite shower room in the master bedroom with a wc is a great selling point for potential renters.

Although a fully tiled bathroom looks very nice, the cost of providing this can impact heavily on your refurbishment budget.

Unless you are prepared to do this work yourself, tiling around sinks and creating a tiled zone around the shower with about a 600mm (2 standard tiles) tiles area around the bathtub is usually sufficient. Using a water repellent gloss emulsion on the rest of the walls will protect the remainder of the plastered surfaces.

Plain white tiles from any major DIY outlet are your best option as, if, any get damaged, the likelihood is that they will still be available from the same outlet.

One nice feature that adds a splash of contrast to any bathroom with a shower fitted is to add a vertical column of tiles centrally behind the taps to give a swath of colour in an all-white room.

As mentioned previously, a brightly coloured, good quality vinyl floor covering adds to the décor. The colour chosen can be matched to the tiling stripe in the shower.

Kitchen

Any family looking to rent or buy any property will always look and desire a nice, sparkling new kitchen as they know this is the one place in which they will be spending a great deal of time.

Therefore, it is important that you make this room a priority in your refurbishment as this can make or break many a rental opportunity.

There is a need to provide sufficient work top space and plenty of cupboard space above and below the work tops.

A 4-ring hob, extractor and a double oven are recommended additions to any kitchen. A nice new and gleaming hob and oven goes a long way to impress the woman of the house either for herself or her husband if he is the main chef in the family.

Provision of white goods is, in the author's opinion, an unnecessary expense as most renters tends to have their own washing machines, fridge/freezer, dishwasher, etc. which they take with them as these items are easily unplugged and moved to the next house. These items, if supplied, can be an extra burden on your maintenance budget as you need to PAT test them plus maintain then replace them when they are broken.

Refurbishment

Leave some open space under the work tops with access to power, water (where required) and drainage so that the tenant can fit their own items into the kitchen.

If you feel you **MUST** supply these types of white goods, never have "fitted" units as they are usually smaller in useful space than freestanding and cost about 50% more to purchase.

The flooring in the kitchen needs to be both waterproof, as spillages are bound to happen, and hard wearing as there is always a lot of foot fall in family kitchens. Ceramic tiling is a nice option but can be more expensive and harder to replace if damaged. They can also be cold in winter and if someone is standing, cooking for any length of time, their feet will get cold.

A good quality cushioned vinyl meets all the above criteria for a great material and also does not get so cold in the winter.

Rent

Chapter 4
Rent

"Landlords grow rich in their sleep."
– John Stuart Mill

Self-manage or Letting Agent?

The first thing to decide when it is time to rent your property is whether to self-manage or to use a good, local letting agent.

Each month or two there seems to be more restrictive legislation imposed from both the government and local authorities with regard to property rental and the role of the landlord in this process. If you are someone who feels that they can keep on top of, understand fully and implement all of these continual changes then the self-manage role is for you!

Also, if you are not local to your rental property (i.e. within a few minutes' drive!) when the tenant locks himself out of the house and rings you to ask for the spare key, are you willing to drive all the way there, open the door and then drive all the way home?

Otherwise consider finding yourself a good and reliable local letting agent.

> **Anecdotal Tale – Self-managing Woes**
>
> One landlord was sitting down with his family for Christmas dinner when he got a call from his tenant, 120 miles away, to say that he had no power and could not cook their meal.
>
> He tried analysing the issue over the phone as his dinner cooled and his wife was giving him daggers, but finally, and after speaking to his local contractor who was unable to help, he ended up driving to the property to discover that the tenant had jammed the wrong coin in the payment slot of his meter requiring a new one which could not be done on Christmas Day.
>
> The tenant therefore went without his Christmas dinner, as did the landlord who had to drive home and face his wife!
>
> As soon as the New Year's festivities were over, he handed his portfolio over to a recommended local letting agent.

Letting Power Team

As with all previous phases of the PRRR process, you will need a power team for lettings consisting of:

- Letting Agent
- General Handyman

Letting Agent

As has been stressed before with your "professional" team members, the chosen company, or your contact in the company, should be an active investor in the same area of property in which you are making your investments.

They will therefore understand your needs as they will align with their own and be ideally suited to be a fully proactive member of your team.

Your relationship with a letting agent can be one of the following:

- Fully Managed Service
- Rent Collection Only
- Tenant Finding Only

Fully Managed Service

This is exactly what it says where the letting agent will do all that is necessary for your property management.

When a tenant is required, they will market your property both locally and nationally, usually on RightMove or OpenRent, interview applicants, carry out all necessary checks, process and hold the deposit in a suitable vehicle and arrange move-in details for the tenant.

They will produce an incoming inventory report with pictures to show the initial condition of the property and which the tenant signs off before moving into the house. This level of detail can save many arguments at the end of a tenancy as there is no evidence against which to make any claims against the deposit.

They will produce, and have signed by the tenant, an Assured Shorthold Tenancy (AST) which outlines the responsibility of both the tenant and the landlord with regard to the property. These are normally for 6 months but can be increased to a 12-month agreement once the tenant is settled and the agent is happy with them.

They will also take the utility readings on the day that the tenant moves in and supply them to the relevant providers along with the new bill holder's name and contact details. They will also inform the local council so that the council tax can be transferred to the new occupier.

Ongoing, once the tenant has moved in, they will collect rents each month and make payment directly to your bank account after deducting their fees. They will also carry out regular inspections to ensure the property is being

Rent

maintained correctly and report back to you. Usually, a first visit is recommended within a month of the tenant taking on the property and then every 3 months is the usual gap. They can request that the tenant carries out any necessary actions if the property is not being kept to the required standard.

As required, they will arrange annual gas checks for the property and the Electrical Installation Condition Report (EICR) every 5 years. A copy of both documents needs to be given to the tenant when they move into the property.

The agent will also be the first point of contact for the tenant on any issues with the property 365/24/7 and be able to organise any remedial works on the property once agreed by you (Also see section on General Handyman below.)

At the end of the tenancy, they will check the property condition against the initial inventory report and either get the tenant to make good any issues and/or withhold some, or all, of the initial deposit to cover repairs.

They will then start the whole process again to fill the property with the least void period, hopefully none. Although this period between tenants can be an ideal opportunity to carry out some minor maintenance on the property so that the new tenants receive the house in pristine condition.

Fully managed fees can range from 8% up to 15% (plus VAT) or more of the monthly rental income but can be a relatively inexpensive way to manage your portfolio.

Rent Collection Only

Here, the agent collects rent as above and also deals with deposit issues, but the rest of the property management is the landlord's responsibility.

This type of service costs around 5% of the monthly rent but is very rarely used by serious property investors.

Tenant Finding Only

This is where the agent finds you a suitable tenant for the property for a one-off fee, usually a month's rent (plus VAT).

They will carry out all the steps outlined under the Fully Managed service up to when the tenant moves in, but here their responsibility ends and it is then the landlord's job to manage the tenant and collect the rents.

This can be a useful service if you do decide to self-manage but don't have the time to keep visiting the property and interviewing tenants.

General Handyman

A good, local handyman can save you a lot of money if they know their stuff.

If there is a problem at your property, and your letting agent is responsible for engaging with tradesmen, there will usually be a minimum call-out charge for the tradesman they send and, if they have made the wrong call, another for the right one to correct the matter.

If you have a local handyman, your letting agent calls them and, for a fixed cost of, say, £20 as agreed, they will visit the property, assess the situation and either sort it out themselves or get the right trade there to do the work.

Letting agents are not always happy with this type of arrangement but it will be up to you to get them to accept the situation. Many agents are now adding on a project manager fee of around 10% on top of the job costs so this is when a handyman can really save you money.

TENANT CHECKS

Common sense would dictate that it is a good idea to carry out a series of checks on an incoming tenant to make sure they can pay the rent on a monthly basis and will be a good tenant.

> **Top Tip**
> **Always do tenant checks.**
> **To protect you and to protect them!**

Up to a few years ago, the tenant was responsible for paying the letting agent or landlord in advance for these checks to be carried out. With the costs running from £40 to £70 and beyond, many tenants declined at this stage as they knew they would fail them, saving both your time and effort in filling a vacancy.

Since the government changed this requirement a few years ago, this cost has fallen on the landlord so it is imperative that you do as much as you can to pre-check the candidates before incurring fees for the checks.

The first thing you need to see from the tenant as a minimum is the last 3 months bank statements (6 months are better if you can get them) so that you can see their regular income from salaries and that their rent has been paid on time each month.

The next check is a reference from their current/last landlord and the landlord previous to last. Remember if they are "problem" tenants, the current landlord might say anything to move them on and make them your problem, not theirs!

If anything looks odd at this point, the recommendation is to call the agent/landlord and see what they say over the phone. You must be very careful what you write about tenants…!

Then you need, if you are happy to proceed, to get a full check through an agency and this should include as a minimum.

- Their job and length of time employed
- Their salary
- Any CCJ (County Court Judgement) against their name and in the case of a couple, against either and both names
- Any adverse credit reports.

If then everything looks OK, you have probably found your tenant.

One further way to protect you when the tenant's income is less than £30k pa is to get a guarantor signed up to the AST for them. This will ensure that any shortfall in rent can be claimed back from them.

Remember, though, to carry out the same set of checks on the guarantor as you did for the tenants.

What Rent Can I Charge?

This always a touchy subject, but you are running a business not a charity so bear that in mind at all times.

There is a minimum rent shown for each type of property by district on every council's web site and this is known as the LHA or Local Housing Authority rates and these are set each year by the government from data collected.

These are very general figures, but when you are doing your initial calculations for suitability, these are the numbers you should use as they "stress test" that the property will work even at these lowest numbers.

Then you need to check the active rents for your area both by postcode and by street name on both the RightMove and OpenRent web sites. This will show you what the local agents are currently charging for similar properties in your particular area.

By now, you will have a full understanding of what existing properties are achieving for rental income, but your property has just been fully refurbished and is in pristine condition. Therefore, you should take advantage of this position and look to charge a small first-let "premium" above the norm.

As was said in the Purchase chapter, by buying the worst house in the street and then refurbishing as outlined in that chapter, you will have set a new standard for property condition and rental so a five to ten per cent premium on the "normal" rents can easily be justified.

Annual Rent Rises

Always make your tenant aware, or make sure the letting agent does the same, that your policy as a landlord is to always increase the rent between 3% and 5% each year on the anniversary of the tenant taking on the property.

By telling the tenant on Day 1, it will not be a complete shock to them on Day 337 when they are told the rent is being increased in 28 days. By knowing well in advance, they can plan and budget accordingly.

> **Top Tip**
> Always increase the rent by as close to 5% each year as can be achieved.

Your reason for annual rent rises at, or near, these percentages is to enable you to refinance every 2 to 3 years, drawing out tax-free cash to use to either buy further properties or to treat you and your family.

The regular rent rises show your lender that the rent is annually aligned and that you will be able to always meet your mortgage payment obligations.

Refinance

Chapter 5

Refinance

"An example of good debt is the debt on the apartment houses I own. That debt is good only as long as there are tenants to pay my mortgages. If tenants stop paying their rent, my good debt turns into bad debt." – Robert Kiyosaki

The importance of regularly refinancing your property portfolio is crucial to enabling you to continue growing your portfolio without the need for any additional funding.

If your goal is, for example, 8 properties all from a single deposit pot and you look to refinance and reuse the cash to buy another property, the model shows that this size of portfolio can be achieved in 9 years as below:

Year 0 – Buy 1 house, assume 8% growth.

Year 3 – Refinance, fund 2nd property deposit.

Year 6 – Refinance, fund 3rd & 4th property deposits.

Year 9 - Refinance, fund 4 more property deposits.

This assumes that you do not use any of your rental monies to speed up the process as each property should bring you in about £250-350 pcm after expenses.

Refinance Power Team

Here you will be using two members of your purchase power team, namely:

- Mortgage Broker
- Solicitor

But on some occasions, and your broker can advise, the mortgage company will include a free solicitor as part of the deal, and this can save you additional funds on refinance and remortgage.

Other People's Money

The great thing about investing in property is that it can be achieved with the use of OPM (Other People's Money) to buy the asset.

If you invest in stocks and shares, gold or even antiques, you will be need to find the full price of the asset when you buy.

Buying property is different as you only need to provide 25% of the cost and your friendly mortgage company or bank will lend you the other 75% allowing you to go off and buy more of the asset type.

They become your silent business partner with a 75% stake in the deal but with none of the benefits you can access, like a share of the monthly rent or a percentage of the refinance deals as you move forward with your portfolio.

When Can I Refinance My Deal?

The current rules seem to stipulate that there needs to be a minimum of 6 months between the original purchase and any remortgage/refinance of the property, but there are a number of mortgage companies who are prepared to shorten this period, enabling you to get your refinance done once the refurbishment is complete and your money out of the deal and onto the next one much quicker.

Your mortgage broker should be able to advise you of a suitable lender and it is best to actually have this conversation before you buy the property rather than after you have invested time and money to then find that you are not able to refinance until six months has elapsed.

Painless Property Investing

In Chapter 2, Purchase, the recommendation was, if you bought with an initial mortgage, to use a product with no Early Repayment Charge (ERC). Although this mortgage might be a little more expensive with a higher rate of interest, you are not locked into the product and required to pay an exit fee to get out of the deal. In some cases, this exit payment can range from £3k to £10k or beyond which can wipe out any benefit in value obtained by all your work so ensure that the mortgage product you use for the initial purchase has no ERC penalty payments. Again, you should have this conversation with your mortgage broker prior to committing rather than once you are in the deal.

In order to qualify for refinance at a significantly higher value to enable you to withdraw your money from the deal, you will have to show the valuer that there has been significant improvements to the property to justify the increase in valuation in such a short period.

Refinance Pack

Prior to starting the process of refinance, you should pull together a valuation, or revaluation, pack comprising the following information:

- Original building survey prior to purchase outlining the areas of the property where work was required.

Refinance

- A list of the major works carried out on the property, with associated costings, to show that any issue in the original survey has been addressed and that improvements have been made to every area of the property
- A series of "before & after" pictures of the property showing the overall improvements that have been undertaken. If you are not going to be onsite during the refurbishment stage, it is imperative that you stress and ensure that your builder/project manager takes detailed pictures of every stage as the work is progressing. Although you may only use a subset of these pictures showing how it was and how it is now, the interim pictures can tell the valuer a story if he has any questions on how the refurbishment was handled.
- Comparable rental figures for similar properties in the area which can be found on the RightMove or OpenRent web sites if you are not planning on putting a tenant into the property before refinance.

Personally, I believe that you should have a tenant in the property as soon as possible and at the maximum rent that you can achieve for the property as, remember, it is like a brand-new house when the tenant takes it over and it will never look as good again, take my word for that.

This shows the valuer when he/she visits that the house is a viable rental property so that the income can be seen to be guaranteed and it also starts bringing you in an income for all the money you have invested in the property to achieve the new value.

Other people I have spoken to will not rent their PRRR properties to tenants until they have achieved refinance as, in their opinion, tenants living in the house will detract from the good work and might even cause the value to be downgraded slightly. This has not been my experience, but the decision to rent or wait will be one that you may have to make.

If your refurbishment has slipped and has consumed most, if not all, of the six months since purchase, you might be best to wait a few days/weeks until the valuer has visited. If you had a future tenant lined up with a signed Assured Shortform Tenancy in place, that is as good as you can get for the valuer.

If you are on top of the works and get the job completed in 2 or 3 months, can you afford to leave the property empty for all that time before refinance? Probably not!

This information pack should be given to your broker to pass on to the mortgage company prior to the valuer visiting the property.

Type Of Mortgage

Your original mortgage, if the property was bought with one, would usually be a standard variable rate product which is not the type required when you refinance. You will now be looking for a fixed rate mortgage for 2 or 3 years maximum.

Why a fixed mortgage and why for only 2 or 3 years?

By choosing a fixed rate mortgage, you tie the rate at the time of purchase, so you have a better grasp on your cash flow. As a variable rate can go up (or down) as the bank lending rate changes, your income for the property can fluctuate accordingly. I appreciate that there have been a few years of minimum interest rates, but the world economy, at the time of writing, is in a tremendous state of flux and fixing what you can now makes good financial sense for the future.

And by fixing for 2 or 3 years, you are then able to take regular advantage of the annual rise in property values to refinance and draw down more tax-free cash that can be used for growing your portfolio or for having a splash out for yourself!

Most investors start with these 2- or 3-year fixed deals when they are growing their portfolios as it gives them money at regular intervals for new deposits for further property acquisitions.

When they feel that they are at a point where their portfolio is of a size that produces an income with which they are happy by replacing, or exceeding, their salary from their JOB (Just Over Broke) then the tendency is to look for a fixed rate for a longer period of 5 to 7 years and let the equity grow in the portfolio for this period.

They may also feel like they need a break from property to travel or to explore other opportunities so by fixing for this longer period, they are free from worry and their incomes are assured while they do something else.

Meeting The Valuer

This first visit by the valuer is very important and should not be left to your local agent or the tenant as this will ultimately determine the amount that you will receive and set you up for your next purchase.

For future valuation visits down the line, you can ask your local letting agent to act for you as, although important, future valuations are not as critical for the well-being and growth of your portfolio as the first one.

If the property is tenanted, you will have to ensure that the tenants are out of the property during this valuation survey. This keeps the story about the property one-dimensional without any asides from the tenant. It will be up to your letting agent to arrange this on your behalf and they should have made the tenant aware when they signed the AST that this would be required.

As stated above, it is recommended that you personally meet the valuer on site and that allows you to have a brief chat, ensure he/she has the valuation report you have already prepared (take a spare copy just in case) and then leave them to their work. In fact, it is best to actually leave the property and wait outside in your car until they have finished or they have any further questions for you.

The reason for leaving the valuer to their own devices is that if you are building a portfolio in a certain area, the likelihood is that you will see the same valuer on your other properties, so it is best not to try and be too friendly with them and keep the matter more business-like!

But if he or she seems chatty and wants to talk that is OK, but don't follow them round the property unless they ask you to accompany them on their tour.

At the end, shake their hand, thank them for their time and try to ascertain when the results might be available. Never ask them for their valuation at that point as they need to sit down and consider all the circumstances before they will determine that number.

Refinance Report

Within a few weeks, you should receive your formal offer from the mortgage company and there should be a copy of the valuation report attached.

When first asking for refinance, and using your knowledge of the local areas and prices, you should have gone for a higher value of more than you needed as this will give the valuer some financial head space in case he feels that this amount is not suitable for your property. Hopefully any downgrading of the price will still leave your mortgage offer as sufficient to draw out your money from the deal.

If he agrees with the amount you have requested, happy days as it gives you back all of the money you wanted to get out of the deal plus a little extra on top.

They say you should always celebrate wins in business as it gets you used to winning so use this extra bit of money to take your team out for a thank you session. I guarantee that they will work all that much harder for you next time!

Rinse & Repeat

Chapter 6

Rinse & Repeat

"How many millionaires do you know who have become wealthy by investing in savings accounts? I rest my case."
– *Robert G. Allen*

So, you have spent the past three to six months working hard to get your first property through the entire PRRR process so what do you do now?

Well, some of you will want to add another R for Rinse and Repeat.

Did you enjoy it? Did you get a real buzz when the valuation exceeded your initial estimates? Do you enjoy seeing a regular income from the rent?

If the answer is YES, you are now ready to start the whole process all over again and put yourself through it all again.

In fact, if you have been enjoying the process and were wanting to do more, the likelihood is that you were already looking around the area for similar properties that could benefit from your expertise. People use guerrilla marketing tactics like leafletting the local streets or a sandwich board outside the property under renovation to attract Direct To Vendor (D2V) deals.

If the answer is NO then you have joined the growing ranks of property investors with a single property as it is estimated that 72% of investors only own 1 property and a further 18% own 2.

That means that only 10% of properties are in the hands of investors owning 3 or more properties. in fact, the survey indicated that only around 1% of investors have portfolios in excess of 6 properties.

This is not to be seen as a slight on your decision, but it just goes to show that many people realise the value of property but find the whole process too difficult to continue with after the first time.

Now, not all of these will have been advocates of the PRRR process and all the work that this entails, some would have bought ready to rent or new-build properties and some would have inherited property from their parents or families.

Whichever is your chosen route now I applaud you.

You gave it a go and it may be something that you want to continue or not, but at least you tried.

By the way, if you are considering selling your single B2L, and it meets the criteria that were set out in the Purchase chapter, drop the author an email as he might be interested in adding it to his portfolio!

Final Thoughts

> *"If you don't find a way to make money while you sleep, you will be working until you die." – Warren Buffett*

Imagine if you, or your parents, had bought the house next door when they bought their family home. By now, they, or you, would probably be able to live off the rent that was being created by the house next door and that is the basis of property investing.

> *"90% of all millionaires became so through owning real estate." – Andrew Carnegie*

Property investing is a great way of creating passive income, but like all other methods, there is still work to be done on your portfolio even when it is set up and running sweetly.

But the work is worth it as it can bring you and your family a good, healthy income to pay for the things you want even if that is more properties.

> *"The wise young man or wage earner of today invests his money into real estate."* – Andrew Carnegie

One way to look at property investment is that it is like growing and nurturing the goose that lays the golden egg as every month, there is the rent paid which is like one gold egg giving a steady income after all bills have been paid.

You then have the real tasty bonuses appearing after every two or three years when the next refinancings are carried out and you see bigger, individual golden eggs being laid for your investment.

And this can, and should continue, even after you've gone, but that requires good tax planning which is beyond the scope of this book.

Final Thoughts

I do hope that you have a serious think about property investing as it has changed the lives of so many people, not all of whom are rich and famous like Lord Alan Sugar or Sir Richard Branson (yes, both of these have sizeable portfolios and enjoy the benefits that brings along with their other business interests)

Don't be surprised when you mention down the pub or the golf club that you are thinking of investing in property, most of your mates will tell you to avoid it at all costs but look for the one who is silent and smiling. Have a chat with him or her when you are alone, and they will probably tell you how well they are doing with their portfolio. And it will probably be the one person you did not think would be that adventurous!

Appendices

Appendix 1 – Six Sources of Seed Capital

There are many ways of funding your first and even subsequent PRRR properties and some are listed below.

PERSONAL SAVINGS

This is the normal starting point where you use your own savings or an inheritance to get started. Most new investors start here and grow slowly.

EQUITY RELEASE FROM YOUR OWN HOME

Many people now have significant equity in their own home and can release the starting funds from this although many lenders are not overly happy when you say that it is for an investment property. So be careful how you tell them the reason for you wanting the money.

FRIENDS AND FAMILY

Friends and family can be a great source of finance as they might have savings not earning them much so you can offer them a few points more than they are getting at the bank to secure their interest and then their money.

Always have a witnessed document showing what you have borrowed, what you will pay back and when the payments will be made.

Remember these people are your friends or your family so it is important that they are fully protected.

JOINT VENTURES

Here you find people outside your circle who have money in savings that is not producing the desired income and they might be willing to lend this money to you for your property purchase.

The deal can be structured in two ways:

- As a loan where you make regular interest payments at a rate above that available at a bank to make it more attractive for an agreed period, usually of five to seven years, at which point the loan is repaid or renegotiated.

- As a joint owner of the property where you share the profits from the rent and from any refinancing in future years

LOANS – PERSONAL AND BRIDGING

This method can be expensive, and you will need to know that the revalued property will cover the cost of the loans if you go this route.

Personal loans can be set up for periods of between three to five years but be wary of any charges if you decide to make an early repayment when you remortgage the property.

Bridging loans tend to be monthly payments of 0.5-1% of the amount borrowed so here you will be paying for the full period until you refinance. The longer this takes, the higher will be your cost of borrowing.

CREDIT CARDS

This method is not for the faint hearted and relies on you being able to keep track of payment dates and finding other interest-free cards that allow credit transfers and cash withdrawals.

This method was very popular when I started out as many houses could be bought for around £20k and it was easy to get a limit of £5k on any number of cards.

With the prices we are discussing you might need to have three or four just for the deposit and a couple more for the refurbishment.

Keeping track is key as any slips in making payments or moving balances to a new card, can bring the whole thing crashing down.

Appendix 2 – The Four Profit Levers In Property Investment

Whenever you purchase a buy to let residential property for investment purposes, there are only four areas where you can make money which are commonly known as the profit levers. This article assumes that you are buying with a mortgage as most property investors do these days.

PROFIT LEVER 1 – DISCOUNT

Whenever you buy an investment property you should always aim to buy with a discount, no matter how small, as this will multiply many-fold over the term of your purchase when in conjunction with profit levers 3 and 4 below.

But it is important that when you do your research on your potential purchase, the numbers stack up even without the discount as you should not rely on the discount you might achieve to bring the purchase into a positive position.

Also, you should do your own due diligence on comparable properties to ensure that any discount achieved is real and is not due to the price being inflated artificially to enable discount.

PROFIT LEVER 2 – RENTAL INCOME

The monthly rental income is the bread and butter of every property investor and is the gift that keeps giving. This is the money that pays all the bills for the property and the balance, after meeting the bills and putting your contingency into a separate account for rainy day issues, is your profit and can be used as wages for you or saved for future investments.

With rental income, it is important to ensure that you are knowledgeable about the local market rents and to ensure that each year you raise the rent by between 3-5% to keep you in a position to enable future remortgaging of the property.

PROFIT LEVER 3 – REFINANCING

Every two to four years, you need to look to remortgage your investment properties with a view to releasing a lump sum income from the additional equity generated on your property,

This is achieved as the UK property market grows steadily and the value of a property doubles, on average, every eight to ten years so you are looking at an annual year-on-year rise of around 8% so after a few years, you can see a significant growth in your property equity.

By drawing out this equity on a regular basis, you receive a tax-free sum which can be used to buy other income-producing assets like more houses and investments or to use some or all of it to treat yourself!

PROFIT LEVER 4 - EQUITY GROWTH

As mentioned above, with the growth in the UK property market, a typical residential property will double in value, thanks to compounding, in around nine years. The equity of 25% that was held initially in the property is retained even with the refinancing activities that will have been carried out.

For a property initially purchased at, say, £100k, there will have been £25k deposit as initial equity equivalent to 25% of the purchase price left in the deal so with the growth in value of the property, this initial 25% will still remain as the equity portion of the growth, but will have also doubled in value to £50k although this money can only be recovered on the sale of the property and would be subject to taxation.

These are therefore the only four areas where profit can be achieved on each and every investment property you buy so when you are doing your due diligence, always do your calculations based on these areas of profit.

Remember – you make your money when you **BUY** a property, not sell it!

Appendix 3 – PRRR and Flipping

A Flip is when you buy a property with the goal of making improvements and selling it with no intention of using it as a rental property. The process then becomes a simple PRR (Purchase, Refurbishment, Resale) exercise as the last step is redundant.

The majority of property investors will buy and hold every property they purchase for the long-term growth in value and the continued monthly rental income.

But there are a small group of people that are involved in the buying and selling of property where they have no intention of holding and renting but are just looking for the regular injection of profits from a quick refurbishment and sale. These do tend to be people already involved in the building trades as their costs are reduced by their ability to do the work rather than pay on top of materials.

When Purchase decision criteria were discussed in Chapter 2, much was made of finding a location where families would be happy to put down roots and stay for the long term. With a flip, the area is not so important only that the research shows that a profit is available and that properties sell quickly without tying up the investor's cash for long periods.

And again, with a flip, the size of the property is not as important as the goal is to purchase, refurbish and sell on as quickly as possible and any property in which a profit can be turned will suffice.

Some investors who operate the buy and hold type of strategy will, occasionally, flip 1 of their purchased properties for a quick cash injection to supplement further purchases.

What To Consider?

Before taking on a flip project, you need to have three vital pieces of information nailed down to ensure that there will be a profit at the end. These are:

1. The End Sales Price
2. Total Costs of Your Refurbishment
3. Overall Timescales

The End Sales Price

When you have identified a possible flip, you should do your due diligence and research sold house prices in that road and up to 2 or 3 roads either side over the past 12-18 months.

Only compare like-for-like properties and, if you are in the area, walk the streets and take note of the relative conditions and any minor changes of these sold properties.

You should also speak to the local estate agents (no more than 2 or 3) as they will be selling the property and ask them for their estimate of the final selling price. Not what they will market the property for, but what they feel they can realistically achieve. At the same time, ask them for some comparables of houses like yours that they have sold over this same period. This will tell you if they are applying some "science" to their numbers or if they are just making a wild guess.

Remember, if you are buying to flip and sell in your own designated rental gold mine area, your knowledge of house prices will probably be greater than most of the estate agents so always bear that in mind when listening to their estimates.

Anyhow, now with all this information to hand, you should be able to get to within +/-5% of what will be the final selling price for the property, and you will need this number to make your final decision when other items are taken into account.

Total Costs of Your Refurbishment

If the property is in your rental gold mine area, it would be better to use a different set of tradesmen for the flip project that for your normal B2L projects. The normal team will be used to working to a slightly lower overall specification on the rental properties, but if you want to achieve a high-priced sale, there will be areas where a higher specification will be required to achieve these top prices.

Here are some specific areas where you should spend more money than for a rental B2L property.

Kitchen – here you will be incorporating brand named quality white goods such as an oven, hob, extraction, washing machine and possibly a tumble dryer and/or a dishwasher. Rather than in a B2L, these should be fitted examples to give nice clean lines as they view the new kitchen.

You may incorporate a large American fridge-freezer as a stand-alone item as this can be a great selling point in a modern looking kitchen.

You might look to a granite or similar worktop and possibly thicker carcasses on the units incorporated in the kitchen.

Flooring – rather than the harder wearing carpet for a B2L, something with a thicker pile should be adopted.

For wet areas, good quality flooring such as Karndean™ can be used which is both hard wearing and waterproof as well as coming in a variety of shades and colours.

As an alternative to carpets in the downstairs rooms, a good quality wooden floor can be laid although this is matter of personal taste.

Bathrooms – A fully tiled bathroom is expected in most homes now so that should be high on your upgrade list. Maybe better quality fittings for the bath and shower, say porcelain rather than plastic for longer life.

These touches, along with tastefully decorated rooms, will add a high degree of quality to the property and again, you are looking for the WOW factor, but this time from someone who is looking to buy rather than rent the property.

Additional costs to take into account against your profit model are items such as

- Council tax
- Mortgage payments

Both will be due monthly whilst you are the owner of the property.

There is also the cost of money to be considered of you are really going to work out the "actual" profit on this deal. If you had not tied up this money in this project, what would it have got you from interest payments?

All of these items need a line in your profit/loss calculations to determine your real profit from the deal (see worked example).

Overall Timescales

When looking at the length of this type of job, it is better to err on the side of longer than you think and then celebrate when it does complete in a shorter period.

Estimating the work required should be relatively easy especially of you have personal experience of these types of jobs or if you are using a trusted contractor for the whole project. Your, or their, number for this should be fairly accurate.

The selling process can be the area where time can slip as probably your buyers are dealing with mortgage companies and with the legal profession. In the main, they are both suspect to lengthy deliberation periods incurring slip in your timescales.

They are also probably having to sell their existing property to move up to yours so there is a chain of people all trying to co-ordinate a suitable set of dates for selling and moving and if you have been involved in one or more of these, you are fully aware of the issues that can arise.

You may have, though, chosen to aim for the first-time buyer where chains are not an issue, but this is the relatively lower priced end of the market. This type of buyer can reduce your overall timescales but

Appendices

can also set a ceiling and therefore a profit level which can be achieved on each flipped property.

A good, average timescale that should be used in your plans is 9 months (what else takes 9 months and is probably as painful for at least one party?) as any shorter would be a tad optimistic.

The ideal would be to start showing the house to prospective buyers in a pre-completed state so that you can:

a) Reduce the overall timescale by finding a buyer and getting them started on their buying process before the work is completed. You can set up a sign in the front garden advertising the property for sale as an easy and quick way to find a buyer.

b) Then you can get the buyer's input on the internal features (tiling, flooring, etc.) where you can get them to pay for higher spec items over and above the prices you were going to spend on the property. The buyer is then upgrading your flip to his specification and paying you for these upgrades in rice. But make sure that this is covered by a contract or even by an EDC agreement (Exchange, Delayed Completion) once they have committed to buy

c) And by selling privately, you would also save on any estate agent fees thereby giving you more money on your bottom line.

Selling The Property

Assuming you are going to use an estate agent, they should be pushed to begin marketing the property before all refurbishment is completed, but after all the dirty jobs and been done. There is nothing worse than a buyer being covered in brick dust as they walk around a property!

But, as was said above, there is nothing to stop you putting a For Sale sign or your own outside the property to drum up some early interest even if you then pass the details to your estate agent for convenience.

Once the estate agent has taken it on board and it is suitable for viewings, make them organize an Open Day on a Saturday at the property and invite as many of their clients who are looking for this type of property to attend. Seeing other people looking around a house can instill some time sensitive issues and push people into moving that little bit faster if they want to secure the property.

And always keep the pressure on the estate agent and, if you can, instruct 2, maybe 3 in total to sell the property as healthy competition is a great thing especially when it is your investment that they are selling!

See the following table that shows the various profit percentages that can be achieved with a typical flip.

Painless Property Investing

Worked Example

	Min	Ave	Max
Projected Sales Price	£100,000	£110,000	£120,000
Refurb Cost	£22,000	£22,000	£22,000
Purchase Costs			
Solicitor	£325	£325	£325
Broker	£325	£325	£325
Sales Costs			
Estate Agent (1%+VAT)	£1,200	£1,320	£1,440
Solicitor	£450	£450	£450
Other Costs			
Insurance	£220	£220	£220
Mortgage (9m)	£675	£675	£675
Council Tax (9m)	£900	£900	£900
Cost of Capital (1%)	£3,000	£3,000	£3,000
Purchase Price	£61,000	£61,000	£61,000
TOTAL ALL COSTS	£90,095	£90,215	£90,335
Cash Profit	£9,905	£19,785	£29,665
% Profit	11%	22%	33%

As can be seen in this worked example, there are significant profits across the board even taking into account the cost of money which most people on projects like this tend to ignore.

I would advise though only to do deals where a minimum profit of 10% can be achieved. Therefore, if the initial sums during your due diligence had determined that the sales price would be in the region of £95,000, this deal would not progress if it was one of mine.

In Conclusion

Flipping properties to create a cash windfall can be a great way to assist with overall cash flow at the start of your property journey.

Always remember though, as highlighted in Appendix Two, The Four Profit Levers In Property Investment, the real wealth in property is gleaned by holding your portfolio for a long time (forever in fact) and taking advantage of refinancing to release tax free cash while still maintaining good equity growth in them.

Appendix 4 – Full Worked Example of One of the Author's PRRR Purchases.

The property in this worked example is a two-bed terraced house located in Salford and built in the 1930's. It was purchased through a sourcing agent as a probate sale but required some modernization and redecorating before it could be let. The estimated value at that time was between £60-65,000.

Purchase price	£48,000
Sourcing costs	£1,800
Solicitor and Survey	£500
Broker fee	£200
Total Purchase Cost	**£50,500**
Refurbishment Cost	**£6,100**

The purchase was achieved with a 75% LTV mortgage of £36,000 with no ERC attached.

On completion of the works, the property was revalued for mortgage purposes at £82,000 which again, at 75% LTV, produced a mortgage of £61,500.

Paying off the first mortgage and covering all expenses including fees of £1,100.00 for this new

Appendices

mortgage gave a tax-free cash sum into my bank balance of £3,800.

As this is a popular area, a tenant was soon found and realized a rental income of £500 pcm and a profit per month after expenses of £395 pcm. Each year the rent was increased by 3% in line with LHA guidelines.

Four years later, the property was again revalued, this time at £100,000 and a new mortgage of £75,000 was achieved. After expenses, a further tax-free cash sum of £11,500 was deposited into my bank.

The rent being achieved by then was £580 pcm with a profit of £460 pcm.

In 2021, the property was again remortgaged at £120,000 to achieve a mortgage of £90,000 which, after paying off the previous mortgage and all expenses gave another £13,500 into my bank account.

The current rental income for this property is £650 pcm with a profit of £530 pcm.

Using the Four Levers from Appendix Two, you can see that this property has generated, for my portfolio, the following impressive numbers.

1. Discount in excess of 20% based on local comparables on purchase.
2. Solid rental income of over £50,000 after expenses in ten years.

3. Refinancing which has created tax free cash income of £28,800 with more to come from future exercises.

4. Equity based on the 25% left in the property of £30,000 up from the original £12,000 on purchase.

So, I think this property, like many others in my portfolio, has followed the tenets of PRRR and has become a PuRRRfect investment for me.

Appendix 5 – Alternative Forced Appreciation Method: Title Split

When browsing the local property pages on the search for another deal, there was a large freehold building for sale which had been converted into 5 1-bed flats and 1 studio flat. The property had been on the market for quite a while and was being put into auction for the second time to see if it could be sold.

On viewing, there were a number of problems (or opportunities for the PRRR investor) in that the ceiling in one flat had collapsed and the flat was inhabitable, a second was in a disgusting state of cleanliness and there was a tenant living there in all his own filth and a third looked as if a whole shelf of paint had exploded and covered all the surfaces.

There was also an opportunity to change the layout and create a 1-bed flat from the studio and a 2-bed flat in the attic from the current 1-bed.

Even with these works and achieving a discount on the asking price, too much money would be left in the deal if it remained as a single freehold, so an alternative plan was hatched.

By creating separate leasehold titles for the 6 flats and maintaining an overall freehold title for the structure, the value of the parts would significantly increase the value of the whole.

The solicitor did all the work for the leases once individual drawings for each flat had been produced so by the time a remortgage was due for the refinance stage, the application was made for six individual mortgages for each of the flats.

The surveyor arrived and had a copy of the original auction offering with her but was suitably impressed by the changes made to the property. With 1-bed flats on the market for £70k and 2-beds for £80k, her valuation of £65k and £75k respectively was a good average offering.

The valuation for the properties was therefore £400k which, at 75% LTV, realized a total of £300k of mortgages. The property and refurbishment cost £185k and the additional legal work was a further £18k giving a tax-free surplus of £97k for further purchases.

The valuation received for a single property had been £220k which would have realized a 75% LTV of £155k leaving around £30k in the property. The title split was easily the best solution for this property.

References

Kiyosaki, Robert	Rich Dad, Poor Dad
Thomas, Dave P	Four Profit Levers in Property Investment - Ezine Articles November 2020
Hardy, Darren	The Compound Effect
Voss, Chris	Never Split The Difference
Michalowicz, Mike	Profit First

One Last Thing...

I would really appreciate it if you would review my book on Amazon and hopefully give me a 5-star rating.

As previously mentioned, I am happy to talk to anyone about property via email to

dave@davethomasproperty.co.uk

I am on Instagram as

@davethomasproperty

Please look me up and follow me for regular property updates and tips.

I can be found on LinkedIn as

https://www.linkedin.com/in/davidthomas992004/

I look forward to connecting with you on any, or all, of the above Social Media channels.

Index

Accidental Landlord, 33
Agent, Letting, 63, 65
Area, Goldmine, 40
Assistant, Virtual, 41
Assured Shorthold Tenancy, 66
Assured Shorthold Tenancy (AST), 66
AST, 66, 72, 85
Buffett, Warren, 25, 93
Builder, 37
Buy To Let (B2L), 14, 19, 26, 91, 106
Carnegie, Andrew, 93, 94
CCJ, 72
Charge, Service, 26
Council Tax, 112
County Court Judgement, 72
D2V, 90
Direct To Vendor, 90
Discount, 116
Distressed Property, 28, 30
Distressed Seller, 28
Divorce, 29
Early Repayment Charge, 43, 80
Equity, 116
Flip, 103
Goldmine Area, 40
Ground Rent, 26
Handyman, 65, 68, 69
Hawley, Brian, 11
HL, 25
HMO, 25
Holiday Let, 14, 25
J.O.B., 84
Jones, Paul, 12
Kiyosaki, Robert, 77
Leeder, Ken, 12
Letting Agent, 63, 65
LHA, 72, 115
Loan To Value, 19
LTV, 19, 36, 114, 118
Mill, John Stuart, 63

Mortgage, 37, 83, 107, 112
  Broker, 37
NMD, 21
No Money Down, 21
No Money Left In, 20
No Money Left In (NMLI), 20
OpenRent, 65, 73, 81
Payne, Chris, 11
Power Team, 37, 64
  Purchase, 37
Probate, 29
Property, Distressed, 28, 30
PRRR, 19, 20, 22, 25, 27, 31, 34, 36, 37, 40, 48, 49, 64, 82, 89, 90, 116, 117
  Cosmetic, 48, 49
  Structural, 48, 50
R2R, 25
Refinance, 19, 27, 75, 77, 79, 80, 86
Relocation, 29
Rent to Rent, 25
Rent, Ground, 26
Repossession, 28
Retirement, 30
Return on Capital Invested, 22
RightMove, 65, 73
ROCI, 22
SA, 25
Seller, Distressed, 28
Service Charge, 26
Serviced Accommodation, 25
Shepard, Sam, 19
Solicitor, 37, 112, 114
Surveyor, 37
Valuer, 84
Virtual Assistant, 41

Printed by Amazon Italia Logistica S.r.l.
Torrazza Piemonte (TO), Italy